Guitar Tab Notebook

THIS BOOK BELONGS TO

_____

_____

Your Journey to Guitar Excellence Begins Here:
Get Your FREE Fretboard Diagram when You Join
Our Newsletter!

https://roden.xyz/go/freegift

If you enjoy this book please consider
telling a friend or giving one as a gift.

Sharing and leaving a review helps us
grow as an independent publisher.

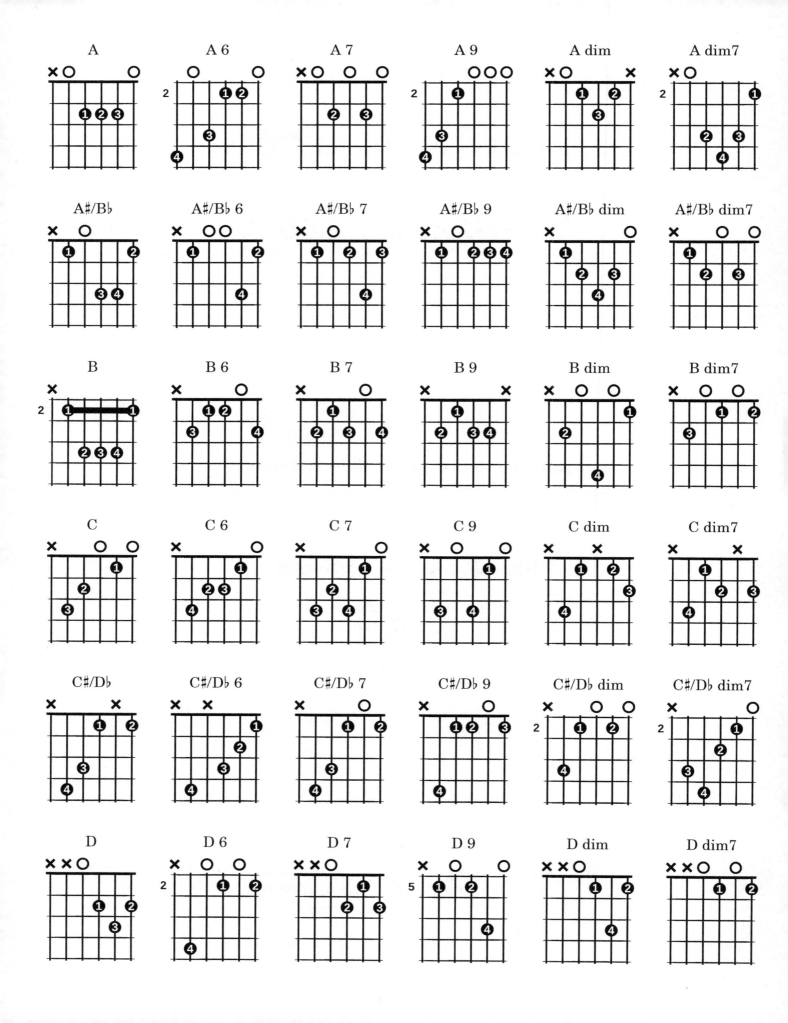

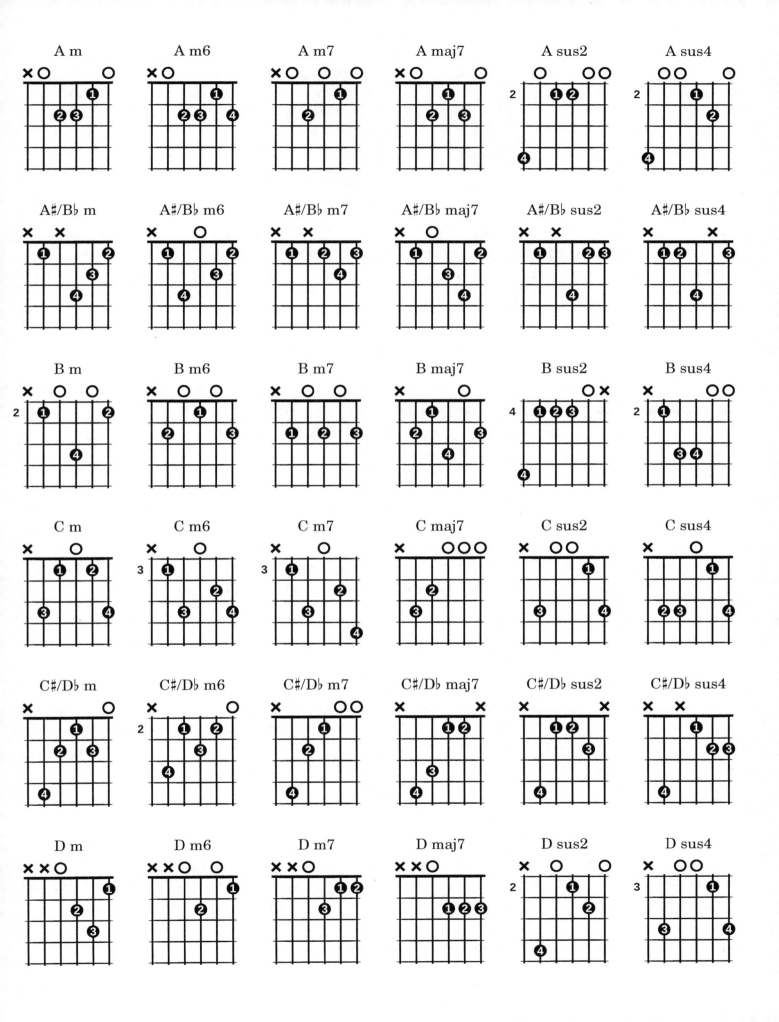

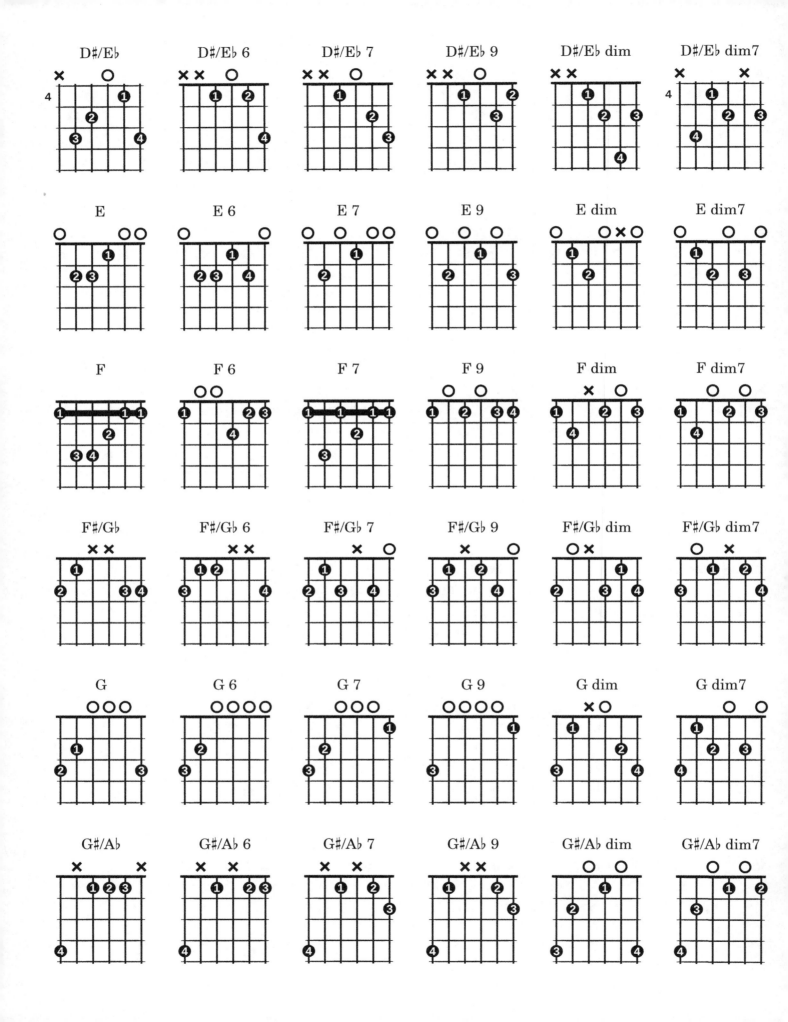

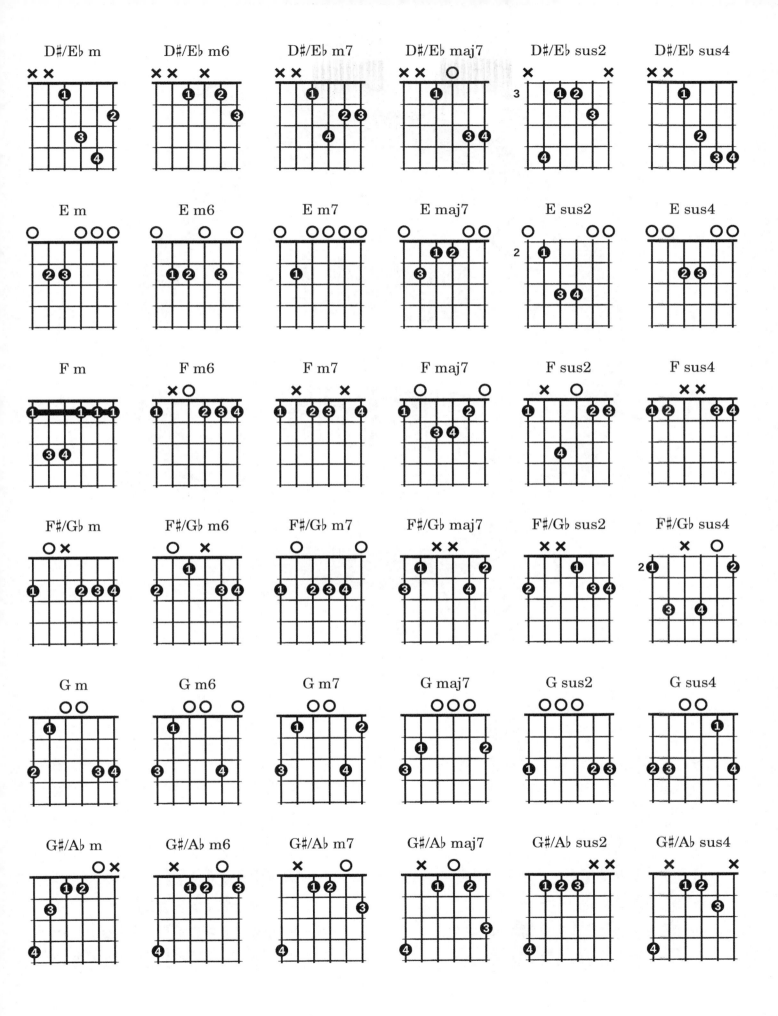

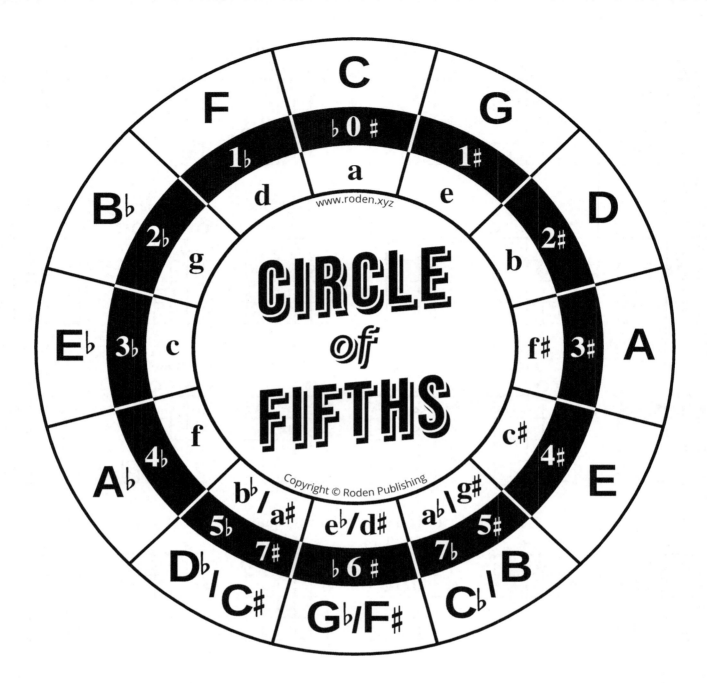

Flats

	B♭	E♭	A♭	D♭	G♭	C♭	F♭	
C	·	·	·	·	·	·	·	a
F	♭	·	·	·	·	·	·	d
B♭	♭	♭	·	·	·	·	·	g
E♭	♭	♭	♭	·	·	·	·	c
A♭	♭	♭	♭	♭	·	·	·	f
D♭	♭	♭	♭	♭	♭	·	·	b♭
G♭	♭	♭	♭	♭	♭	♭	·	e♭
C♭	♭	♭	♭	♭	♭	♭	♭	a♭

Sharps

	F#	C#	G#	D#	A#	E#	B#	
C	·	·	·	·	·	·	·	a
G	#	·	·	·	·	·	·	e
D	#	#	·	·	·	·	·	b
A	#	#	#	·	·	·	·	f#
E	#	#	#	#	·	·	·	c#
B	#	#	#	#	#	·	·	g#
F#	#	#	#	#	#	#	·	d#
C#	#	#	#	#	#	#	#	a#

TAB

TAB

TAB

TAB

TAB

TAB

TAB

```
┌─┬─┬─┐   ┌─┬─┬─┐   ┌─┬─┬─┐   ┌─┬─┬─┐   ┌─┬─┬─┐   ┌─┬─┬─┐
├─┼─┼─┤   ├─┼─┼─┤   ├─┼─┼─┤   ├─┼─┼─┤   ├─┼─┼─┤   ├─┼─┼─┤
├─┼─┼─┤   ├─┼─┼─┤   ├─┼─┼─┤   ├─┼─┼─┤   ├─┼─┼─┤   ├─┼─┼─┤
├─┼─┼─┤   ├─┼─┼─┤   ├─┼─┼─┤   ├─┼─┼─┤   ├─┼─┼─┤   ├─┼─┼─┤
└─┴─┴─┘   └─┴─┴─┘   └─┴─┴─┘   └─┴─┴─┘   └─┴─┴─┘   └─┴─┴─┘
```

T
A
B

T
A
B

T
A
B

T
A
B

T
A
B

T
A
B

T
A
B

T
A
B

T
A
B

T
A
B

T
A
B

T
A
B

T
A
B

T
A
B

T
A
B

T
A
B

T
A
B

T
A
B

T
A
B

T
A
B

T
A
B

T
A
B

T
A
B

T
A
B

T
A
B

T
A
B

T
A
B

T
A
B

```
T
A
B
```

```
T
A
B
```

```
T
A
B
```

```
T
A
B
```

```
T
A
B
```

```
T
A
B
```

```
T
A
B
```

```
T
A
B
```

```
T
A
B
```

```
T
A
B
```

```
T
A
B
```

```
T
A
B
```

```
T
A
B
```

```
T
A
B
```

```
T
A
B
```

```
T
A
B
```

```
T
A
B
```

```
T
A
B
```

```
T
A
B
```

```
T
A
B
```

```
T
A
B
```

TAB

```
T
A
B
```

```
T
A
B
```

```
T
A
B
```

```
T
A
B
```

```
T
A
B
```

```
T
A
B
```

```
T
A
B
```

```
T
A
B
```

```
T
A
B
```

```
T
A
B
```

```
T
A
B
```

```
T
A
B
```

```
T
A
B
```

```
T
A
B
```

```
T
A
B
```

```
T
A
B
```

```
T
A
B
```

```
T
A
B
```

```
T
A
B
```

```
T
A
B
```

```
T
A
B
```

T
A
B

T
A
B

T
A
B

T
A
B

T
A
B

T
A
B

T
A
B

```
T
A
B


T
A
B


T
A
B


T
A
B


T
A
B


T
A
B


T
A
B
```

T
A
B

T
A
B

T
A
B

T
A
B

T
A
B

T
A
B

T
A
B

This page is a blank guitar tablature template. It contains six empty chord diagram grids at the top, followed by seven blank TAB staves.

```
T
A
B
```

```
T
A
B
```

```
T
A
B
```

```
T
A
B
```

```
T
A
B
```

```
T
A
B
```

```
T
A
B
```

```
T
A
B
```

```
T
A
B
```

```
T
A
B
```

```
T
A
B
```

```
T
A
B
```

```
T
A
B
```

```
T
A
B
```

```
T
A
B
```

```
T
A
B
```

```
T
A
B
```

```
T
A
B
```

```
T
A
B
```

```
T
A
B
```

```
T
A
B
```

T
A
B

T
A
B

T
A
B

T
A
B

T
A
B

T
A
B

T
A
B

```
T
A
B
```

```
T
A
B
```

```
T
A
B
```

```
T
A
B
```

```
T
A
B
```

```
T
A
B
```

```
T
A
B
```

T
A
B

T
A
B

T
A
B

T
A
B

T
A
B

T
A
B

T
A
B

T
A
B

T
A
B

T
A
B

T
A
B

T
A
B

T
A
B

T
A
B

```
T
A
B


T
A
B


T
A
B


T
A
B


T
A
B


T
A
B


T
A
B
```

```
T
A
B
```

```
T
A
B
```

```
T
A
B
```

```
T
A
B
```

```
T
A
B
```

```
T
A
B
```

```
T
A
B
```

```
T
A
B


T
A
B


T
A
B


T
A
B


T
A
B


T
A
B


T
A
B
```

```
T
A
B
```

```
T
A
B
```

```
T
A
B
```

```
T
A
B
```

```
T
A
B
```

```
T
A
B
```

```
T
A
B
```

```
┌─┬─┬─┬─┐   ┌─┬─┬─┬─┐   ┌─┬─┬─┬─┐   ┌─┬─┬─┬─┐   ┌─┬─┬─┬─┐   ┌─┬─┬─┬─┐
├─┼─┼─┼─┤   ├─┼─┼─┼─┤   ├─┼─┼─┼─┤   ├─┼─┼─┼─┤   ├─┼─┼─┼─┤   ├─┼─┼─┼─┤
├─┼─┼─┼─┤   ├─┼─┼─┼─┤   ├─┼─┼─┼─┤   ├─┼─┼─┼─┤   ├─┼─┼─┼─┤   ├─┼─┼─┼─┤
├─┼─┼─┼─┤   ├─┼─┼─┼─┤   ├─┼─┼─┼─┤   ├─┼─┼─┼─┤   ├─┼─┼─┼─┤   ├─┼─┼─┼─┤
├─┼─┼─┼─┤   ├─┼─┼─┼─┤   ├─┼─┼─┼─┤   ├─┼─┼─┼─┤   ├─┼─┼─┼─┤   ├─┼─┼─┼─┤
└─┴─┴─┴─┘   └─┴─┴─┴─┘   └─┴─┴─┴─┘   └─┴─┴─┴─┘   └─┴─┴─┴─┘   └─┴─┴─┴─┘
```

T
A
B

T
A
B

T
A
B

T
A
B

T
A
B

T
A
B

T
A
B

T
A
B

T
A
B

T
A
B

T
A
B

T
A
B

T
A
B

T
A
B

```
T
A
B
```

```
T
A
B
```

```
T
A
B
```

```
T
A
B
```

```
T
A
B
```

```
T
A
B
```

```
T
A
B
```

T
A
B

T
A
B

T
A
B

T
A
B

T
A
B

T
A
B

T
A
B

T
A
B

T
A
B

T
A
B

T
A
B

T
A
B

T
A
B

T
A
B

T
A
B

T
A
B

T
A
B

T
A
B

T
A
B

T
A
B

T
A
B

TAB

TAB

TAB

TAB

TAB

TAB

TAB

```
T
A
B


T
A
B


T
A
B


T
A
B


T
A
B


T
A
B


T
A
B
```

T
A
B

T
A
B

T
A
B

T
A
B

T
A
B

T
A
B

T
A
B

```
T
A
B
```

```
T
A
B
```

```
T
A
B
```

```
T
A
B
```

```
T
A
B
```

```
T
A
B
```

```
T
A
B
```

```
T
A
B
```

```
T
A
B
```

```
T
A
B
```

```
T
A
B
```

```
T
A
B
```

```
T
A
B
```

```
T
A
B
```

```
T
A
B
```

```
T
A
B
```

```
T
A
B
```

```
T
A
B
```

```
T
A
B
```

```
T
A
B
```

```
T
A
B
```

```
T
A
B
```

```
T
A
B
```

```
T
A
B
```

```
T
A
B
```

```
T
A
B
```

```
T
A
B
```

```
T
A
B
```

```
T
A
B
```

```
T
A
B
```

```
T
A
B
```

```
T
A
B
```

```
T
A
B
```

```
T
A
B
```

```
T
A
B
```

T
A
B

T
A
B

T
A
B

T
A
B

T
A
B

T
A
B

T
A
B

TAB

TAB

TAB

TAB

TAB

TAB

TAB

```
T
A
B
```

```
T
A
B
```

```
T
A
B
```

```
T
A
B
```

```
T
A
B
```

```
T
A
B
```

```
T
A
B
```

```
┌──────┐   ┌──────┐   ┌──────┐   ┌──────┐   ┌──────┐   ┌──────┐
│┼┼┼┼┼│   │┼┼┼┼┼│   │┼┼┼┼┼│   │┼┼┼┼┼│   │┼┼┼┼┼│   │┼┼┼┼┼│
└──────┘   └──────┘   └──────┘   └──────┘   └──────┘   └──────┘
```

T
A
B

T
A
B

T
A
B

T
A
B

T
A
B

T
A
B

T
A
B

T
A
B

T
A
B

T
A
B

T
A
B

T
A
B

T
A
B

T
A
B

T
A
B

Blank chord diagram and tablature worksheet.

Six blank chord diagram grids across the top.

Seven blank tablature staves labeled:

T
A
B

```
T
A
B
```

```
T
A
B
```

```
T
A
B
```

```
T
A
B
```

```
T
A
B
```

```
T
A
B
```

```
T
A
B
```

Printed in Great Britain
by Amazon